Keyboard Meditations

Devotional Selections
for the
Piano Soloist

Arranged by DON PHILLIPS

Lillenas PUBLISHING COMPANY
KANSAS CITY, MO 64141

Contents

We Will Glorify

TWILA PARIS
Arranged by Don Phillips

Fairest Lord Jesus

Traditional
Arranged by Don Phillips

Reverently ♩= ca. 72

I Exalt Thee

PETE SANCHEZ, JR.
Arranged by Don Phillips

Nothing but the Blood of Jesus

ROBERT LOWRY
Arranged by Don Phillips

Expressively ♩ = ca. 72

More Precious than Silver

LYNN DESHAZO
Arranged by Don Phillips

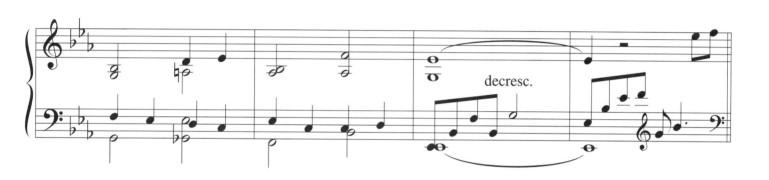

A little faster

Freely

I Am Thine, O Lord

WILLIAM H. DOANE
Arranged by Don Phillips

Tenderly ♩ = ca. 68

O Lord, You're Beautiful

KEITH GREEN
Arranged by Don Phillips

With devotion ♩ = ca. 88

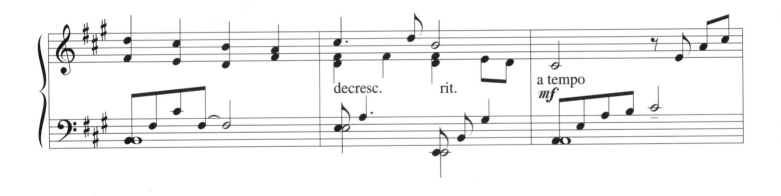

Wonderful, Wonderful Jesus

ERNEST O. SELLERS
Arranged by Don Phillips

Expressively ♩ = ca. 96

Spirit Song

JOHN WIMBER
Arranged by Don Phillips

Reverently ♩ = ca. 72

His Eye Is on the Sparrow

CHARLES H. GABRIEL
Arranged by Don Phillips

Tenderly, freely ♩ = ca. 84